Fish from the Sea

Geoffrey Patterson

ANDRE DEUTSCH

To Rosamund Inglis

FISH FROM THE SEA

Introduction

The sea is a wonderful larder full of good things to eat. There are many many different kinds of fish and shellfish. Seaweeds, too, are plentiful and are used to make cosmetics and medicines. They are also excellent in soups and as 'vegetables'.

Like all other creatures, fish need to breed, or they will die out. That is why there are times in the year when you can't buy a particular kind of fish unless it is frozen. When they are ready to spawn (lay their eggs) female fish have thousands of tiny eggs called roe in their bodies. If they are caught before they have had time to release the eggs into the sea then the eggs will not grow, there will be no new fish and the numbers of fish in the sea will get fewer and fewer. Some fish, particularly herring and haddock, have in the past been caught during their breeding season, with the result that fishermen found their catches getting smaller and smaller.

But if we look after the sea and the fish that live in it properly, it will always give us a rich and varied supply of food.

Next time you go to the sea, try to imagine what is happening below the waves.

First published in 1988 by
André Deutsch Limited
105-106 Great Russell Street, London WC1B 3LJ

British Library Cataloguing in Publication Data

Patterson, Geoffrey
Fish from the sea.
1. Fish – For children
I. Title
597

ISBN 0 233 98272 8

Mackerel

Many of the fish and most of the shellfish that live in the sea make good food. Some, like sharks and tunny fish, are huge. Some, like sprats and shrimps, are tiny. Some thrive in cold water, some prefer warm seas.

Different kinds of fish swim at different depths in the ocean. The ones found not far under the waves, like the silvery-blue mackerel in this picture, are called 'pelagic', which simply means that they live in the open sea, not at the bottom.

Fish, especially smaller ones, swim together in shoals. Sometimes hundreds, even thousands, keep close to each other as they move through the water. This is their way of protecting themselves from the large fish that prey on them.

Cod

Fish that live deeper in the sea, a little above the sea-bed, are known as 'Demersal' species. 'Round Demersal' fish, like the cod shown here, can grow to a weight of 80lbs (36 kilos). Demersal means living near the bottom of the sea, and 'round' describes their rounded, tube-shaped bodies.

Cod live in the cold waters of the North Atlantic Ocean. They are such good food, and so plentiful, that great fleets of fishing boats can spend weeks at sea catching them. We need to be careful not to catch too many, though, if they are to survive.

There are many other members of the cod family: haddock, pollock, whiting, coley and ling are just a few.

Plaice

At the very bottom of the sea, on the sandy, pebbly sea-bed, live fish called 'Flat Demersals' like this orange-speckled plaice. 'Flat' because they are almost flat. Their sandy, speckly bodies make it difficult for the fish who prey on them to spot them. Both their eyes are on the same side of their heads, looking up — and looking out for danger. When it comes they wriggle into the sand and are almost invisible.

Some other flat fish are Dover sole, lemon sole, giant halibut and the turbot.

Both round and flat demersal fish are called 'white fish' by fishmongers, and they are all good to eat.

John Dory
Whiting
Red Bream
Sprat
Hake

Turbot
Skate
Bass
Monk Fish
(Angler Fish)
Squid

Lobster

Fish covered with a hard shell are called shellfish. Some of the most common, shrimps, prawns, crabs and lobsters belong to a family called 'crustaceans', which means 'covered with a crust'.

Crabs and lobsters are caught in pots or creels called lobster pots. These are often made of steel, and covered with wire or plastic netting.

There is an entrance hole through which the crab or lobster crawls to get at the left-over scrap of fish inside, called bait. Once inside, it is trapped by the shape of the pot, the shape of which varies according to the choice of the fisherman.

Crabs and lobsters live on the sea-bed, in fairly shallow water near the coast. The fisherman baits the pot and lowers it to the sea-bed. The line fastened to the pot sometimes has pieces of cork placed along it; it's position in the sea is always marked by a brightly coloured marker, which bobs in the waves and helps the fisherman to find his pots easily.

Mussels, cockles, oysters, limpets and scallops, which also have shells to protect them, belong to a family called molluscs. Mollusc is a word used to name a creature that is soft-bodied (has no skeleton), is all in one piece and is usually covered with a hard shell.

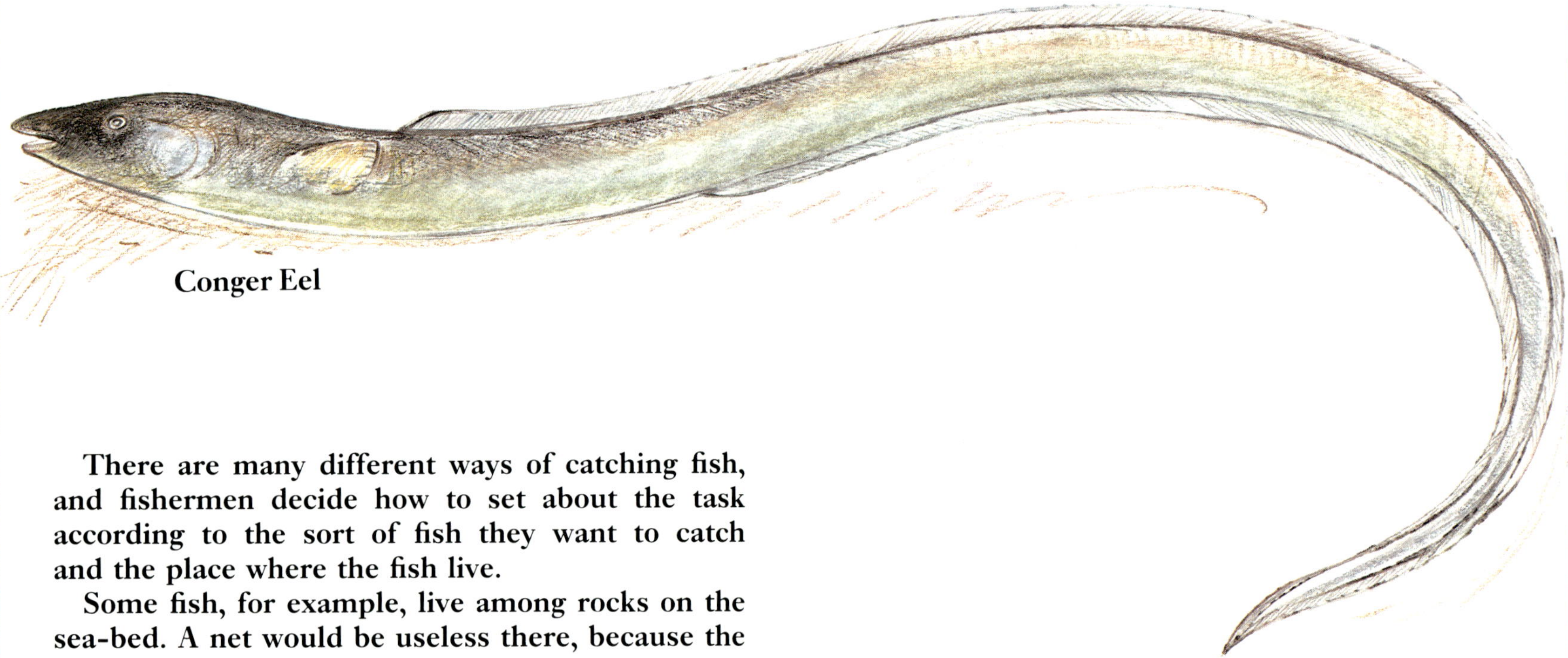

Conger Eel

There are many different ways of catching fish, and fishermen decide how to set about the task according to the sort of fish they want to catch and the place where the fish live.

Some fish, for example, live among rocks on the sea-bed. A net would be useless there, because the jagged rocks would tear it, so they are sometimes caught with a 'long-line'.

Getting a long-line ready is hard work because it has a great many hooks, all of which must be baited and tied securely to a line of enormous length (at times over a kilometre), each hook about a metre or more apart. The line is then taken to the place where the fishermen want to fish and cast into the water to lie on the sea-bed. Small anchors stop the line from drifting, and marker buoys show the fisherman where it is. The line is left in the water for a few hours, then hauled back into the boat.

Although this sort of fishing is hard work, fish caught on a long-line earn more money for the fisherman, due to their high quality.

Cod, mackerel, haddock and dog fish are some of the fish that can be caught round coasts in this way.

Long line hook

Haddock

Though many fishing boats are made of steel and fibre glass, plenty of fishermen would prefer them to be built of wood, if it were not now expensive and hard to get. Fishing boats have to be very strong and able to stand up to the rough seas they may meet on a long trip, searching for fish in all weathers.

The skipper in charge of the boat and his men have to be tough, too, and willing to work in cold weather at any time of the day or night.

Some fishing boats, which go out only for hours at a time, or a day or two at most, stay close to the coast and are quite small. Others can be as much as 70 to 100 metres long. These stay away from home for weeks and are like floating factories, where fish are gutted and deep-frozen, all before they reach land.

In this picture a trawler is shooting out a net or 'trawl' made of nylon to catch fish on the sea-bed.

MORISTON
LT62

Dover Sole

A 'trawl' is a net, nowadays made of man-made fibres, which is dragged over the sea-bed by the trawler, scooping up fish as it goes.

Metal doors at the front of the net are pushed open by the water as the trawler moves forward. As long as the net moves forward, the doors will hold the mouth of the net open.

The top edge of the net has floats attached to it to help keep it open. Weights and sometimes rollers are attached to the bottom edge, so the net moves smoothly over the sea-bed just above the bottom. As it goes it disturbs the water and the sand, forcing the fish to swim up from the bottom and fall back into the moving net.

A trawl is used to catch fish like plaice, sole, halibut, turbot, cod, haddock, whiting and many others.

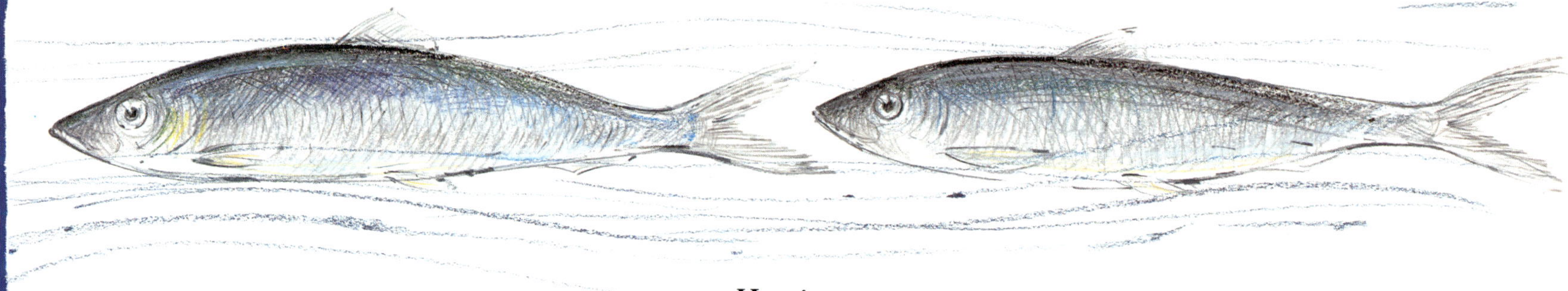

Herring

Trawls can also used to fish in deep water well above the sea-bed. These pelagic trawls do not have rollers as they never touch the bottom. They are mostly used to catch herring and mackerel. The fish swim into the open mouth of the net and are forced to the bag-like end (known as the cod end) by the rush of water. A full net stretches out, rather like a sock.

As trawlers have become more powerful and nets larger, so catches have got bigger. It is hard for fish to reproduce themselves fast enough to keep up with the appetites of people all over the world who enjoy fish. If young fish are to grow into adults and produce young, then they must escape the trawls – the mesh must be large enough to enable them to slip through. Rules about mesh sizes are now enforced in many countries, and fishermen who break the rules are punished with heavy fines.

When the trawl is winched back on board the end of the net away from the mouth is opened, and the fish pour out onto the deck for sorting. Many kinds of fish may have been caught in the trawl and they must be sorted before anything else is done. On a big trawler, or factory ship, the holds are refrigerated. The fish are packed and deep frozen in blocks. This means a deep sea trawler can stay at sea for weeks and still bring back fish in perfect condition.

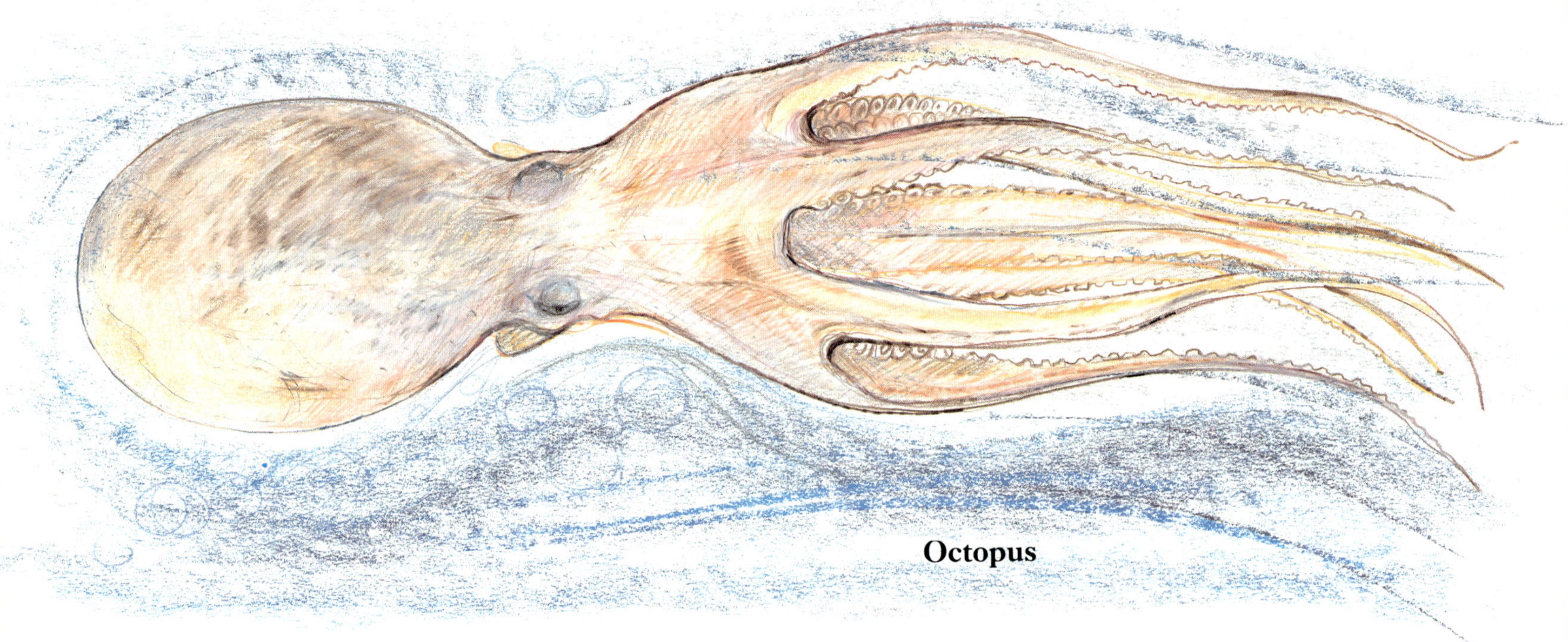

Octopus

On small trawlers where there is no deep freezer, fish are gutted as soon as the net is hauled on board. The crew, wearing rubber gloves, boots and oilskins to protect them from the weather, gut the fish and pack them in ice. Fish packed in ice are called 'wet fish', and are not deep frozen. They cost more in the market or the fishmonger because they are fresh. The crews of these small trawlers work fast, balancing on rolling decks and using sharp knives, so they must be as skilled at this job as they are at handling full trawls.

If the catch has been a good one, as soon as the net is emptied it goes back into the sea, and the crew set to work on the gutting, sorting and packing. No wonder they get little rest on a successful trip.

Red Mullet

When fishing boats reach port their catch is taken to huge sheds on the dockside and usually displayed in baskets or plastic or wooden boxes. People who make their living out of fish come from all over the country to buy them, usually at an auction. At an auction buyers walk round the shed inspecting the fish carefully. They have to make sure that the kind of fish their customers need are there, and that they are in good condition. If they are happy with the quality of the trawler's catch, then they offer what they think it is worth. The one who offers the most is the successful buyer.

Buyers have to be on their toes at a sale. Prices are shouted out very fast and it is easy to miss the chance to buy.

At a big fish auction a great variety of fish is displayed; white fish, such as cod, lemon sole, whiting, plaice and haddock; less plentiful fish like halibut, turbot, John Dory or even octopus and squid. There will also be a good supply of shellfish from prawns and shrimps – which may well go to frozen food factories on their way to the supermarkets – to whelks and cockles for the street corner stall.

Crab

If you live in a town where there is a good fishmonger, or even a mobile fish shop that comes once a week, you are lucky. A fishmonger not only chooses his fish carefully, making sure it is fresh, but also has many varieties to make your choice more interesting, and takes the trouble to display them carefully. Many fishmongers put out their fish on a marble slab; they prefer marble because it is cool, easy to clean and looks attractive.

When you eat fish you are enjoying a meal which not only tastes good but is rich in protein and minerals such as calcium and iodine which your body needs. Oily fish, like mackerel and herring, are particularly good because they contain vitamin A, which helps you to stay healthy, and vitamin D which you need to build strong bones.

54.
FRESH FISH
54.
OPEN
PUSH

Mussel

If you visit your local fishmonger you might see the fish he has for sale displayed like the ones in this picture. Fish are best eaten fresh, although frozen fish fingers are popular and make a quick and easy meal. In the list on this page and page 30 the months shown beside each type of fish are those when they are most plentiful.

Flat Demersal – White Fish

	Season
Brill	June – February
Dab	Sept – May
Flounder	March – November
Halibut	June – March
Megrim	May – March
Plaice	May – February
Skate	May – February
Lemon & Dover Sole	May – March
Turbot	April – February
Witch	May – February

KIPPERS
£1·25
PER lb.
FINNAN
HADDOCK
£1·85 PER lb.
COD
STEAKS
£2·20
PER lb.
CRAB
FLAVOURED
STICKS
13p EACH
GREY
MULLET
£1·20 PER lb
LEMON
SOLE
£2·10
PER lb.
WHITING
FILLETS
£1·25
PER lb.
MACKEREL
85p
PER lb.

Scallop

Queen Scallop

Round Demersal – White Fish

Bass	August – March
Cod	June – February
Conger Eel	March – October
Coley	August – February
Haddock	May – February
Hake	June – March
Huss	All Year
John Dory	All Year
Ling	Sept – July
Red Mullet	May – November
Grey Mullet	Sept – February
Pollock	May – September
Sea Bream	June – February
Whiting	June – February

Oily Fish

Herring	May – December
Mackerel	All Year
Sprat	Oct – March

Shellfish

Cockles	May – December
Crab	April – December
Lobster	April – November
Mussels	Sept – March
Oysters	Sept – April
Scallops	Sept – March
Shrimps	Feb – October
Whelks	Feb – August
Squid	May – October

INDEX

The author acknowledges with gratitude the help received from the following in the preparation of this book, George Cable of Aldeburgh and Mr Fred Smith.